Made in United States
Troutdale, OR
12/06/2024

25989282R10070